WINDOWS 11

FOR BEGINNERS 2024

EMPOWER YOUR COMPUTING JOURNEY

By

Dennis Charles

COPYRIGHT

Printed in the United States of America
© 2023 by Dennis Charles

New Age Publishing
USA | UK | CANADA

TABLE OF CONTENTS

INTRODUCTION

Have you ever sat before a computer screen, feeling like an explorer lost in a dense jungle of pixels and icons? Each mouse click sends you deeper into the wild world of technology, filled with mysterious languages and perplexing symbols. Fear not, dear reader, for I am here to guide you through this virtual jungle and introduce you to the captivating wonders of Windows 11.

Imagine stepping into a sparkling wonderland, where each digital window is a portal to infinite possibilities. Windows 11, like a vibrant tapestry woven from the threads of innovation and simplicity, beckons even the most hesitant of beginners to embrace the unknown and embark on a journey of discovery. As we embark on this enchanting adventure together, allow me to unveil the secrets of this new and captivating operating system.

At first glance, the sight of Windows 11 may overwhelm the uninitiated. A symphony of vibrant colors dances across the screen, inviting you to explore its depths. But fear not, my dear novice, for beneath this seemingly complex facade lies a gentle simplicity that will guide you through the labyrinthine corridors of the digital realm.

Picture yourself standing amid a serene meadow, sunlight streaming through a canopy of leaves above, gently caressing your face with warmth. This is the sensation Windows 11 offers to those who dare to venture into its vast expanse. Its sleek design, with rounded corners and soft edges, calls to mind the gentle curves of a babbling brook meandering through a lush valley. And just as the brook whispers its soothing melody, Windows 11 whispers in your ear, assuring you that the mysteries of technology are not as impossible as they may seem.

As we delve deeper into this virtual utopia, we will encounter the magical realm of the Start Menu. Like a treasure chest filled with digital gems, it presents a world of possibilities with just a single click. No longer confined to a rigid grid, this redesigned Start Menu welcomes you with open arms, inviting you to arrange and personalize your most cherished apps and shortcuts. It becomes a canvas upon which you can paint your digital masterpiece, reflecting your unique personality and preferences.

But Windows 11 has more to offer than just a visually satisfying experience. I invite you to imagine yourself stepping into a grand library, its shelves brimming with knowledge from every corner of the globe. In this digital incarnation, Windows 11 presents many tools and features designed to enhance productivity and make life easier. From the new Snap Layouts that allow you to effortlessly organize multiple windows to the Virtual Desktops that lend a touch of magic to your multitasking endeavours, this operating system is like a loyal companion, always ready to lend a helping hand.

In our journey through Windows 11, we will also encounter the enchanting world of Microsoft Store. Like a bustling marketplace in the heart of a medieval village, it offers a cornucopia of applications and tools, each waiting for you to discover its hidden potential. Whether you seek entertainment, knowledge, or the means to express your creativity, the Microsoft Store is a treasure trove you can browse with the excitement of a child in a toy store. There is no end to the adventures that await you here, dear novice.

Now, I know what you may be thinking. How can one possibly navigate this vast terrain without getting lost? What if I make a wrong turn or stumble upon a hidden obstacle? Fear not, gentle reader, for I am here as your trusty guide. With each turn of the page, I will be by your side, offering explanations and gentle nudges in the right direction.

So, my dear beginners, starters, and novices, prepare yourselves for an enchanting journey through the captivating world of Windows 11. We will embark on an adventure filled with wonder, simplicity, and endless possibilities. Through my words, let me be your guide as we navigate this virtual jungle full of excitement and discovery. And remember, dear reader, the realm of

Windows 11 is waiting to welcome you with open arms, eager to reveal its secrets and unlock a world of boundless potential. Let our journey begin!

CHAPTER 1: GETTING STARTED WITH WINDOWS 11

UNDERSTANDING THE WINDOWS 11 INTERFACE

The Start Menu

Let's begin with the Start menu, which has undergone a significant redesign in Windows 11. When you first boot up your PC, you'll notice the Start button in the screen's lower left corner. This button is your gateway to accessing all the apps and features that Windows 11 offers. Clicking on it will open up the Start menu, which is now centered on the screen and features a clean and minimalist design.

Within the Start menu, you will find various options to explore. At the top, you'll see a search bar, allowing you to find and launch specific apps or search the web quickly. Below the search bar, you'll find the "Recommended" section, which displays frequently used apps and recent documents, making accessing your most essential tools easier.

Moving further down the Start menu, you'll see your installed application list. This list is divided into two sections: "Pinned" and "All apps." The Pinned section displays your favorite or most frequently used apps, which you can customize to suit your preferences. As the name suggests, the All apps section presents a comprehensive list of all the applications installed on your PC.

To the right of the Start menu, you'll notice a series of Live Tiles. These tiles provide real-time information and updates from certain apps, such as weather forecasts, news headlines, or calendar appointments. These Live Tiles can be personalized, resized, and rearranged to suit your needs and display the information that matters most.

The Taskbar

Now that we've explored the Start menu, let's turn our attention to the taskbar, which is the bar located at the bottom of the screen. The taskbar in Windows 11 has also undergone some changes compared to previous versions, aiming to provide a cleaner and more streamlined experience.

Starting from the left, you'll find the Task View button. Clicking on this button allows you to see all your open windows and switch between them effortlessly. It provides a helpful visual overview of your current activities, making multitasking a breeze.

Next is the new Start button, which we have already covered when discussing the Start menu. This button provides a quick way to access the Start menu from the taskbar itself, offering a convenient alternative to clicking in the center of the screen.

Moving along, you'll come across the Microsoft Edge icon, which gives you instant access to the default web browser. Having the browser easily accessible on the taskbar lets you browse the internet without launching it from the Start menu or desktop.

Continuing towards the right, you'll find the new system tray. The system tray houses various icons, providing quick access to essential system functions and information. Some common icons in the system tray include the volume control, network connection status, battery level (for laptop users), and the date and time.

The Action Center

Lastly, we come to the Action Center at the far-right corner of the taskbar. Clicking on the Action Center brings up a panel filled with notifications and quick settings for various system features. Notifications can come from various sources, such as Windows updates, new emails, or app updates. You can access more details or take action directly from the Action Center by clicking on a notification.

Below the notifications, you'll find the quick settings area, providing toggles for commonly used features such as Wi-

Fi, Bluetooth, airplane mode, and screen brightness. These quick settings give you easy control over your device's essential functions, allowing you to make quick adjustments on the fly.

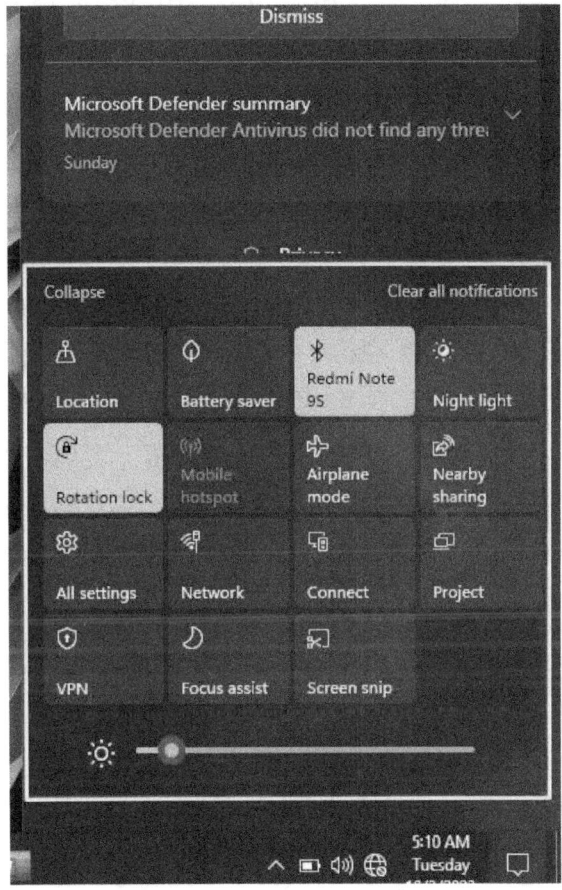

You can also access additional settings in the Action Centre by clicking on the "All settings" button. This will take you to the full Settings app, where you can customize and personalize your Windows 11 experience to your heart's desire.

By understanding the different elements of the Windows 11 interface, including the Start menu, taskbar, and Action Center, you will be equipped with the knowledge needed to navigate the system effortlessly and access its various features and functions. Take your time to familiarize yourself with these elements and make them work for you, as they are the gateway to a smooth and efficient Windows 11 experience.

As a beginner, exploring and becoming comfortable with the Windows 11 interface is just the beginning of your journey into the world of this operating system. From here, you can dive deeper into specific features, learn more about customization options, and discover how to optimize your workflow. Windows 11 has a lot to offer, and by understanding its interface, you will be well on your way to mastering this powerful operating system.

CUSTOMIZING YOUR WINDOWS 11 EXPERIENCE

Desktop Background

Let's begin with the first step: customizing the desktop background. Your desktop background is the first thing you see when you log in to your computer, so choosing an image that resonates with you is essential. Windows 11 offers a wide range of pre-installed images that you can choose from or select your favorite image from your photo library. To change your desktop background, right-click on an empty area of your desktop and select "Personalize" from the drop-down menu. This will open the Personalization settings panel, where you can customize various aspects of your Windows 11 interface. Click "Background" and choose the desired image from the available options. You can also select a slideshow of multiple images if you prefer. Don't forget to click "Apply" to save your changes.

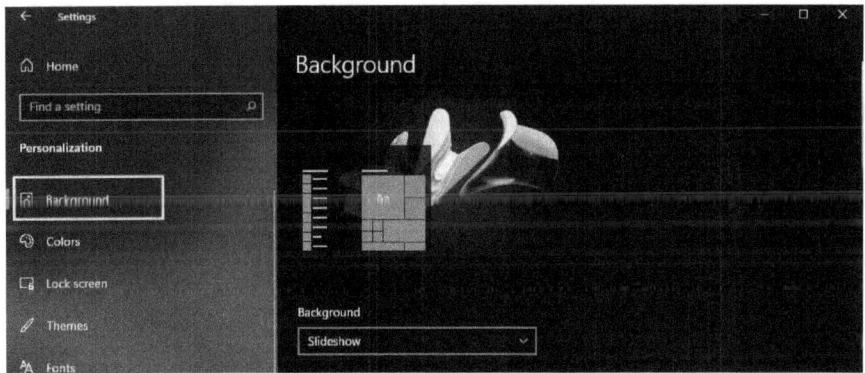

Theme

Moving on to the next step, let's explore how you can customize the theme of your Windows 11. The theme includes elements such as window colors, desktop icons, and mouse cursor styles. To access the theme settings, go back to the Personalization settings panel (right-click on an empty area of your desktop and select "Personalize" from the drop-down menu) and click on "Theme." Here, you will find a list of pre-installed themes that you can choose from. Each theme offers a unique combination of colors and styles to suit different preferences. If you want to create your custom theme, click "Customize your theme" at the bottom. This will open the Colors and Appearances settings panel, where you can manually select different colors for your windows, buttons, and other interface elements. You can also customize the mouse cursor and the size of text and icons. Once you are happy with your changes, click "Apply" to save the new theme.

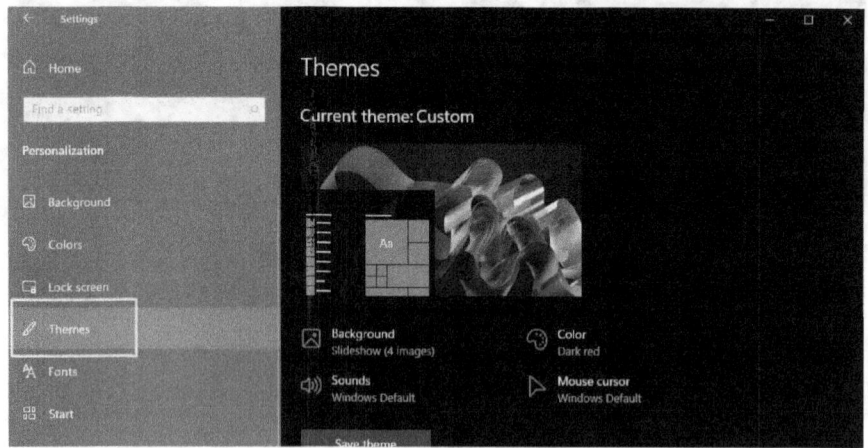

System Settings

Now that we've covered the basics of customizing the desktop background and theme, let's delve into the realm of system settings customization. Windows 11 allows you to tweak various system settings to optimize your computer's performance and adapt it to your needs. To access the system settings, click the Start button and select "Settings" from the menu. You will find many options to customize your Windows 11 experience in the Settings window. Here are a few key system settings that you may want to consider adjusting.

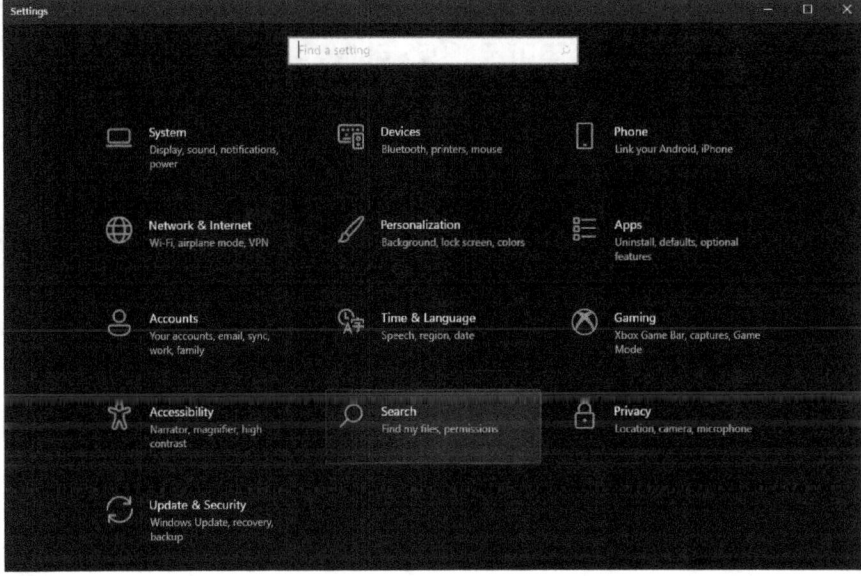

First, explore the "Personalization" category in the Settings window. Here, you can fine-tune settings related to your desktop, taskbar, and Start menu. For example, you can choose whether or not to show the date and time on the taskbar, select how taskbar buttons are grouped, and even enable or disable the Live Tiles feature on the Start menu.

These small adjustments can significantly impact your overall Windows 11 experience by making it more efficient and tailored to your preferences.

Next, move on to the "Accounts" category in the Settings window. Here, you can manage your account settings, including personalizing your profile picture and changing your account password. You can also sync your settings across multiple devices by enabling the "Sync settings" option. This ensures that your personalized Windows 11 experience is consistent across all your devices, making it easier to transition between them seamlessly.

Let's explore the "System" category in the Settings window. Here, you will find various options to customize your computer's behaviour and performance. For example, you can adjust the display scaling to make text and icons more legible on high-resolution screens. Depending on your needs, you can also configure the power settings to optimize battery life or performance. Additionally, you can customize the default apps for various file types and protocols, ensuring that your favorite apps are always ready to open the files you use most frequently.

Finally, let's not forget about the "Accessibility" category in the Settings window. Windows 11 offers a range of accessibility features that can enhance your computer experience if you have specific needs or preferences. From enabling color filters to assist with color vision deficiencies to adjusting text size and contrast for better readability, these accessibility options can make Windows 11 more inclusive and user-friendly for all users.

As you can see, Windows 11 offers many customization options to personalize your desktop background, theme, and system settings. By exploring these options and making the necessary adjustments, you can create a Windows 11 experience that truly reflects your unique style and preferences. So go ahead, dive into the world of customization, and make Windows 11 your masterpiece.

NAVIGATING AND ORGANIZING FILES AND FOLDERS

Step 1: Opening File Explorer

To begin, you need to open the File Explorer. There are multiple ways to do this, but the most common method is to click the "File Explorer" icon on the taskbar. Alternatively, you can use the keyboard shortcut by pressing the "Windows key" + "E".

Once File Explorer is open, you will be greeted with a window that displays your system's Libraries, drives, and folders. The new layout in Windows 11 offers a clean and minimalist interface, making it easier for beginners to navigate through their files.

Step 2: Understanding the File Explorer Interface

Before we dive deeper into the navigation and organization aspects, let's familiarize ourselves with the File Explorer interface. At the top of the window, you will find the Ribbon, which contains multiple tabs such as "File," "Home," "Share," and "View," each offering different commands and options related to managing files.

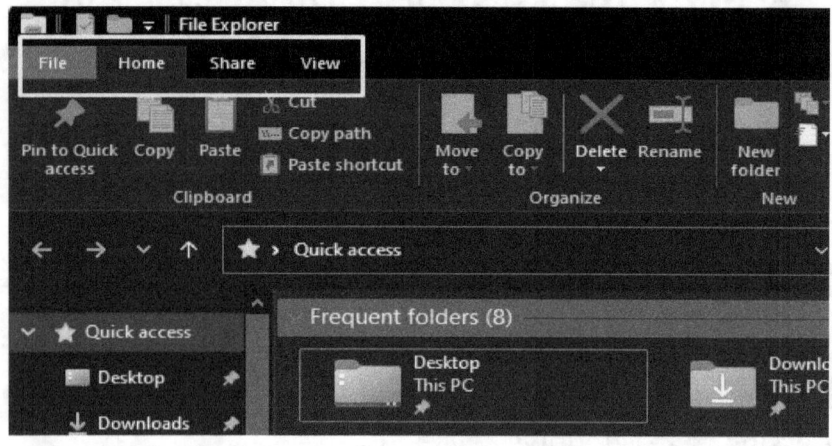

Underneath the Ribbon, you will notice a toolbar that includes common functions such as "Copy," "Paste," "Delete," and "Properties." These tools will be useful when performing different actions on your files and folders.

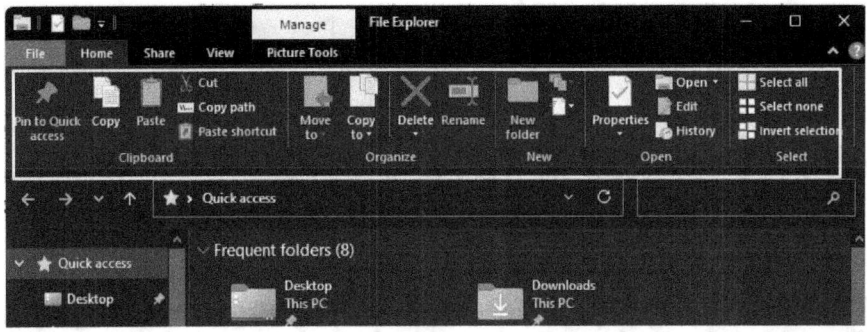

In the main section of the window, you will see the file and folder contents of the currently selected directory. Each file or folder is represented by an icon, making it easier to distinguish between different file types visually. By default, File Explorer displays files and folders in a tiled view, but you can adjust the view settings according to your preference.

Step 3: Navigating Folders

Now that you understand the File Explorer interface, let's dive into the navigation aspect. To move between folders, you can double-click on a folder to open it. To go back to the previous directory, you can either use the "Back" button situated in the toolbar or press the "Alt" + "Left Arrow" keyboard shortcut.

If you want to navigate to a specific directory quickly, use the address bar at the top of the window. Clicking on the arrow next to the current folder's name will open a drop-down menu displaying the full path of the current directory. You can click on any folder within the path to navigate directly to it.

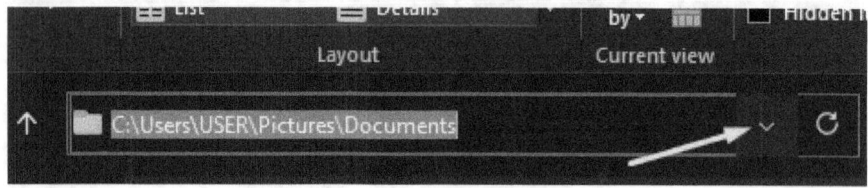

Step 4: Searching for Files and Folders

In Windows 11, searching for files and folders is a breeze. The search bar at the top right corner of the File Explorer window allows you to quickly search for specific files or folders by typing in keywords or file names. As you type, Windows 11 will instantly filter the search results, making it easier to locate the desired item.

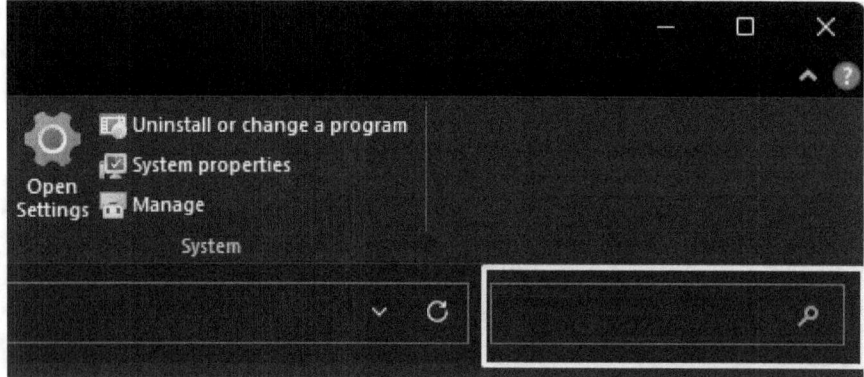

You can also refine your search by using filters such as file type, size, and date modified. To access these filters, click the "Search" tab in the Ribbon and select the desired options from the drop-down menu. These search filters will help you narrow your search results and find the files and folders you're looking for more efficiently.

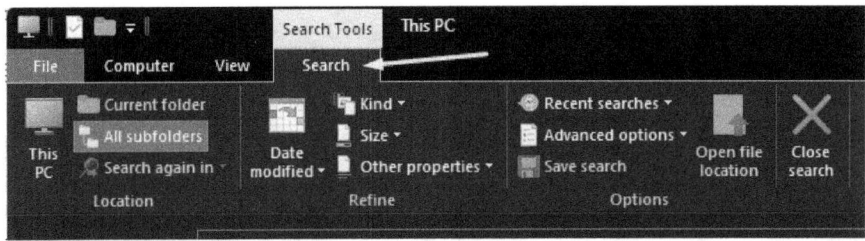

Step 5: Organizing Files and Folders

Now that you have mastered navigating through your files and folders, let's explore different ways to organize them effectively. Windows 11 offers various tools and features to help you keep your files in order, making it easier to find what you need when you need it.

One of the most powerful features of File Explorer is the ability to create new folders. To create a new folder, navigate to the directory where you want the new folder to be and click on the "New Folder" button in the toolbar. You can then give the new folder a descriptive name and start populating it with relevant files.

To keep your files better organized, you can also take advantage of the "Quick Access" feature in Windows 11. Quick Access is a section in the File Explorer sidebar that displays your most frequently used folders and recently accessed files. To add a folder to Quick Access, right-click on it and select "Pin to Quick Access." This allows you to quickly access important folders without navigating multiple directories.

Another helpful feature is "File and Folder Properties," which provides additional information and customization options. To access properties, right-click on a file or folder and select "Properties" from the context menu. In the Properties dialogue box, you can view details such as file size, creation date, and permissions. You can also customize the appearance of folders and files by changing their icons or adding tags for easier identification.

In addition to these features, Windows 11 offers advanced options for organizing files and folders, such as grouping and sorting. By right-clicking on the empty space within the File Explorer window and selecting "Group by" or "Sort by" options, you can arrange your files based on criteria such as name, size, type, and date modified. This makes it easier to find specific files or quickly identify duplicates.

Step 6: Advanced Navigation Techniques

Lastly, explore some advanced navigation techniques to enhance your productivity further. One such technique is using keyboard shortcuts to navigate through File Explorer quickly. Windows 11 provides many keyboard shortcuts for file management tasks, such as copying, pasting, renaming, and deleting files. Learning these shortcuts can significantly speed up your workflow and save you time.

Additionally, you can customize the File Explorer layout and view settings according to your preferences. By right-clicking on the empty space within the File Explorer window and selecting "Customize" from the context menu, you can change the default view, adjust column widths, and choose which details to display for files and folders.

Conclusion:

In conclusion, navigating and organizing files and folders in Windows 11 is a breeze with the enhanced features of File Explorer. By following the step-by-step guide and utilizing the various tools and features available, readers can efficiently explore their files, stay organized, and manage their computers effectively. Whether you are a beginner or an experienced user, mastering these skills will undoubtedly enhance your Windows 11 experience and improve productivity. So, dive in and confidently begin exploring the wonders of file navigation and organization!

CHAPTER 2: MASTERING WINDOWS 11 PRODUCTIVITY TOOLS

ENHANCING EFFICIENCY WITH THE TASKBAR AND START MENU

Step 1: Customizing the Taskbar

The first step towards harnessing the power of the Taskbar is to customize it according to your personal preferences and workflow. Windows 11 offers a multitude of options to tweak and modify the Taskbar to suit your needs. To begin, right-click on an empty area of the Taskbar, and a menu will pop up, offering a range of customization options.

One of the most useful features is the ability to pin your favorite apps to the Taskbar. This eliminates the need to search for applications every time you want to access them, saving valuable time and effort. To pin an app, open it, right-click its icon in the Taskbar, and select "Pin to Taskbar." You can also rearrange the order of the pinned apps by clicking and dragging them to your desired position.

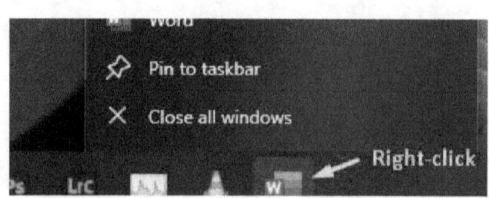

Another handy customization option is the ability to choose how icons are displayed on the Taskbar. By right-clicking on an empty area of the Taskbar and selecting "Taskbar settings," you can navigate to the "Taskbar behaviors" section. Here, you'll find options to combine taskbar buttons, hide or show labels for running apps, and even choose whether to display the Taskbar on multiple monitors.

Step 2: Utilizing the Start Menu

Now that we have customized the Taskbar to our liking, let's dive into the functionalities of the Start menu. Windows 11 introduces a visually appealing and highly functional Start menu, combining the best aspects of the classic Start menu and the Live Tiles from Windows 10.

To access the Start menu, click on the Windows icon at the far left of the Taskbar. From here, you can browse through your installed apps, recent documents, recommended files, and even perform quick searches. The Start menu offers a seamless and efficient way to access your most frequently used applications and files.

One of the standout features of the Start menu in Windows 11 is the ability to pin specific documents or files for quick access. To pin a file, locate it in File Explorer, right-click on it, and select "Pin to Start." The file will now appear as a tile in the Start menu, allowing you to open it with just a click quickly. This feature is handy for files you need to access frequently, such as documents for ongoing projects or spreadsheets with live data.

Step 3: Mastering Taskbar and Start Menu Shortcuts

To truly enhance efficiency and streamline your workflow, it is essential to master the various shortcuts and hotkeys associated with the Taskbar and Start menu. Windows 11 offers a wide range of keyboard shortcuts that can save you precious time and energy, once you get accustomed to them.

Here are some of the most useful shortcuts to boost your productivity:

- Win + T: This shortcut allows you to cycle through the apps in the Taskbar, giving you instant access to the programs you need without even lifting your hand from the keyboard.

- Win + 1-9: By pressing the Windows key along with a number key, you can open the corresponding app on the Taskbar. For example, pressing Win + 1 will open the first pinned app on the leftmost position of the Taskbar.

- Win + A: This shortcut opens the Action Center to access various system settings and notifications.

- Win + D: By hitting this shortcut, you can quickly minimize all windows and go straight to the desktop, allowing you to access files and folders effortlessly.

- Win + S: Pressing this combination will open the Search bar, enabling you to perform quick searches for apps, documents, settings, and more.

These are just a few examples of the many shortcuts available in Windows 11. Once you familiarize yourself with these time-saving key combinations, you'll wonder how you managed without them.

Step 4: Task View and Virtual Desktops

Windows 11 introduces a revamped version of Task View, a feature that allows you to view and manage all open windows in a visually appealing manner. By clicking on the Task View icon in the Taskbar or pressing Win + Tab, you can enter the immersive Task View mode, where you can see all open windows as individual tiles.

Task View is beneficial when working on multiple projects simultaneously or when you need to switch between applications frequently. You can switch to the desired app by simply clicking on a tile, eliminating the need to navigate through multiple windows or cluttered desktops.

Furthermore, Windows 11 introduces the concept of virtual desktops, an innovative feature that allows you to create multiple desktops for different purposes. This functionality is especially beneficial for individuals who work with numerous applications or need to maintain distinct workspaces. To create a virtual desktop, click the Task View icon and select "New Desktop" at the top of the screen. You can then switch between desktops by clicking on the corresponding tiles in Task View.

Step 5: Focus Assist and the Notification Area

To truly enhance productivity, it is crucial to minimize distractions and interruptions. Windows 11 offers an invaluable feature called Focus Assist, which allows you to customize and manage notifications according to your needs. By right-clicking on the Action Center icon in the Taskbar and selecting "Focus Assist," you can enable this feature and choose from various options such as priority-only, alarms only, or even automatic rules based on your activity.

Additionally, the Notification area in the Taskbar provides quick access to essential system notifications and settings. By clicking on the clock icon in the Taskbar, you can view the date and time and access the Calendar, Battery settings, and other handy shortcuts.

In conclusion, the Taskbar and Start menu in Windows 11 offer a wealth of features and customization options that can significantly enhance efficiency and productivity. By customizing the Taskbar, utilizing the Start menu effectively, mastering shortcuts, exploring Task View and virtual desktops, and managing Focus Assist, you can easily streamline your workflow and access frequently used applications and files. Embrace the power of Windows 11 and witness firsthand its impact on your productivity.

HARNESSING THE POWER OF WINDOWS 11 SEARCH

Introduction:

In today's digital age, information is at our fingertips. We can access a wealth of knowledge, files, and applications with just a few clicks. However, the challenge lies in efficiently finding what we need amidst the vast sea of data. Windows 11, with its improved search capabilities, aims to solve this problem by providing users with advanced techniques for harnessing the power of search. In this chapter, we will delve into the intricacies of Windows 11 Search and explore how readers can optimize their search experience. From quickly finding files to customizing search settings, this step-by-step guide will empower beginners to become proficient in mastering Windows 11's search functionality.

Overview of Windows 11 Search

To fully tap into the potential of Windows 11 Search, it's crucial to understand its fundamental aspects. Windows 11 Search allows users to effortlessly sift through files, settings, and applications. The search bar on the taskbar serves as the gateway to this powerful feature. A simple click or tap on the magnifying glass icon opens up a world of possibilities.

The Basics of Windows 11 Search

Before delving into advanced search techniques, it's essential to have a solid grasp of the basics. Windows 11 offers several ways to initiate a search, including typing directly into the search bar, using keywords, or scanning through the search results. By familiarizing ourselves with these fundamentals, we lay the foundation for more complex search operations.

Typing in the Search Bar

The search bar is the gateway to all search activities in Windows 11. Users can quickly find files, settings, or applications by typing directly into the search bar. Windows 11's intelligent search feature suggests relevant results as the user types, allowing for a seamless and efficient search experience.

Utilizing Keywords

Keywords are the backbone of effective searches. Windows 11 Search recognizes specific keywords that help narrow down search results. By using keywords such as "filetype:", "date:", or "size:", users can refine their searches to pinpoint the exact information they are looking for. This technique is particularly handy when dealing with large volumes of data or when searching for specific file types.

Scanning Through Search Results

Windows 11 presents search results in a clear and organized manner. Users can quickly identify the file or application they seek by scanning the search results. The preview pane provides a glimpse into the content of each result, enabling users to verify its relevance before opening or accessing it. This approach saves time and enhances productivity.

Advanced Techniques for Windows 11 Search

Building upon the basics, we can now explore advanced techniques that enable users to fully harness the power of

Windows 11 Search. By employing these techniques, readers will become proficient in unlocking the full potential of this robust feature.

Customizing Search Settings

Windows 11 allows users to customize search settings to align with their individual preferences. By navigating to the Settings menu, readers will discover many options for personalizing their search experience. From choosing which folders to include in search results to adjusting indexing options, these settings empower users to tailor their search results to meet their specific requirements.

Searching Within Files

Sometimes, the information we need is buried within a document or file. Windows 11's advanced search capabilities enable users to search within files, saving precious time. By typing the relevant keywords into the search bar and selecting the "Search within files" option, users can narrow down their search to the content within files, ensuring that no vital information goes unnoticed.

Conclusion:

Harnessing the power of Windows 11 Search is a skill that allows users to efficiently navigate through the vast amounts of information available on their devices. By familiarizing themselves with the basics, embracing advanced techniques, and leveraging customization options, readers will unlock the true potential of Windows 11's search capabilities. This chapter has armed beginners with a comprehensive step-by-step guide to mastering Windows 11 Search, paving the way for enhanced productivity and ease of use in their digital endeavors.

MAXIMIZING MULTITASKING WITH VIRTUAL DESKTOPS

Step 1: Understanding Virtual Desktops

To begin our journey, let's first grasp the concept of virtual desktops. Imagine having multiple screens dedicated to a specific task, all within a single physical screen. With virtual desktops, you can create different workspaces to categorize your projects and switch between them seamlessly. No longer will you feel overwhelmed by a cluster of open windows; instead, you will have a clear and organized digital workspace.

Step 2: Creating Your First Virtual Desktop

Now that we understand the concept of virtual desktops, let's dive into the practical steps of creating and managing them. To create your first virtual desktop, follow these straightforward steps:

1. Click on the Task View icon, represented by a square icon next to the search bar on the taskbar.

2. You will be presented with a stunning mosaic of your open windows, resembling a bird's eye view of your digital universe. At the top of this view, you will see a "New Desktop" option. Click on it, and voila! You have created your first virtual desktop.

3. You can now switch between your virtual desktops by clicking on the Task View icon and selecting the desktop of your choice.

Step 3: Customizing and Managing Your Virtual Desktops

Once you have created multiple virtual desktops, learning how to customize them to suit your specific needs is essential. Here are some features and tips to help you optimize your virtual desktops:

1. Personalizing Desktop Names: To avoid confusion, especially when dealing with numerous virtual desktops, renaming them according to the tasks or projects they represent can be incredibly helpful. To do this, simply hover over the desktop in Task View, click on the three dots that appear, and select "Rename."

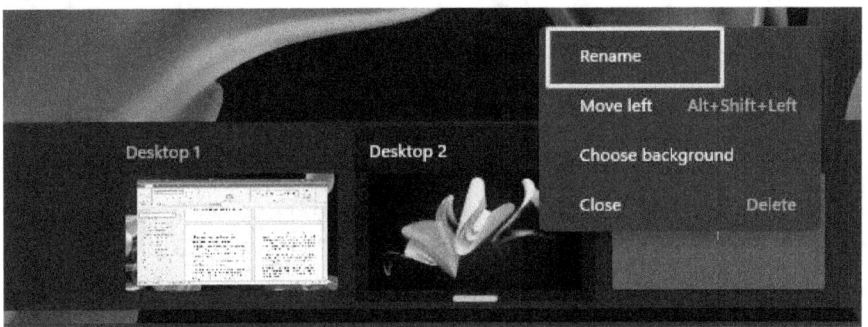

2. Moving Windows Between Virtual Desktops: Sometimes, you may realize that you've opened a window in the wrong virtual desktop. Thankfully, Windows 11 allows you to move windows seamlessly between desktops. To do this, right-click on the desired window's title bar and select the "Move to" option. From there, you can choose the virtual desktop to which you wish to transfer the window.

3. Keyboard Shortcuts: To enhance efficiency, Windows 11 offers several keyboard shortcuts to navigate between virtual desktops swiftly. Some popular shortcuts include:

- Windows Key + Ctrl + D: Creates a new virtual desktop

- Windows Key + Ctrl + Left/Right Arrow: Switches between virtual desktops

- Windows Key + Ctrl + F4: Closes the current virtual desktop

4. Closing Virtual Desktops: Once you've completed a task on a specific virtual desktop, it's time to close it to avoid clutter. To do this, enter Task View, hover over the desired desktop, click on the three dots, and select "Close."

Step 4: Utilizing Task View to Manage Open Windows

Task View is a powerful tool that allows you to create and manage virtual desktops and provides an overarching view of all your open windows. In this step, we will explore some key features of Task View and ways to optimize your multitasking capabilities:

1. Closing Individual Windows: From Task View, you can close specific windows without closing the entire virtual desktop. Hover over the desired window and click on the "X" button that appears at the top right corner.

2. Moving Between Windows: Task View enables you to navigate between open windows sleekly and intuitively. To switch between windows, click on the desired window in Task View, and it will become the active window.

3. Additional Task View Options: Task View offers a range of additional options to enhance your multitasking

experience. For instance, you can select multiple windows simultaneously by holding down the Ctrl key while clicking on them.

Step 5: Expanding Multitasking with Snap Assist

Snap Assist is another feature in Windows 11 that complements virtual desktops by allowing you to snap windows into organized layouts. With Snap Assist, you can effortlessly arrange your windows side by side, creating an ideal workspace for multitasking. Here's how to leverage Snap Assist:

1. Snap Windows Together: To snap windows side by side, drag them to opposite edges of the screen until you see a transparent overlay indicating the placement. Release the window, and it will snap into place. You can repeat this process with additional windows, creating a multi-window layout.

2. Resizing and Adjusting Windows: Once you have snapped windows together, you can resize them to your liking. Hover over the dividing line between two windows, and a two-headed arrow cursor will appear. Click and drag the cursor to adjust the size of each window.

3. Creating Window Grids: For even more control over your multitasking environment, you can use Snap Assist to create window grids. To do this, snap the first window into place, then select another window and drag it to the

central area of the screen until you see a 2x2 grid overlay. Release the window, and it will automatically arrange into a grid layout.

Achieve Multitasking Mastery

Congratulations! By mastering virtual desktops and exploring additional tools like Task View and Snap Assist, you have unlocked the true potential of multitasking in Windows 11. With your newfound knowledge, you can effortlessly juggle multiple projects, seamlessly switch between tasks, and create an organized workspace that fosters productivity like never before.

Remember, practice makes perfect while utilizing virtual desktops and other multitasking features. So, feel free to experiment, personalize, and adapt these tools to fit your unique workflow. Windows 11 is your canvas, and the possibilities are limitless. Happy multitasking!

CHAPTER 3: EXPLORING WINDOWS 11 ESSENTIAL APPS

MASTERING THE MICROSOFT EDGE WEB BROWSER

In this subchapter, we will explore the realm of Microsoft Edge, exploring its tab management, extensions, and privacy settings. These key elements will help you make the most out of your browsing experience and keep your online activities secure and private.

Tab Management

Let's begin with tab management. When you open Microsoft Edge, you are greeted with a sleek, minimalist interface that encourages a clutter-free browsing experience. Tabs are the building blocks of your browsing session, and Edge provides several efficient ways to manage them.

One of the most useful features is the ability to set aside tabs. Imagine you are working on a project, researching different topics, and suddenly, you must switch gears and focus on something else. Instead of closing all the tabs and losing your progress, you can set them aside. This neat feature allows you to group related tabs and quickly access them later, ensuring that your browsing session remains organized and efficient.

To set aside tabs, you can click on the three-dot menu at the top right corner of the browser and select "Set these tabs aside." Alternatively, you can use the keyboard shortcut Ctrl + Shift + T. When you're ready to revisit your set-aside tabs, click on the tab preview button next to the address bar, and you'll find all your saved tabs neatly grouped and waiting for you.

Extensions

Extensions are another powerful tool that can enhance your browsing experience in Microsoft Edge. These add-ons or plugins allow you to customize and personalize your browser to match your specific needs. Whether it's blocking annoying ads, managing your passwords, or boosting your productivity, there is an extension for nearly every purpose.

To access extensions in Microsoft Edge, click on the three-dot menu, go to "Extensions," and then select "Get extensions from the Microsoft Store." The Microsoft Store offers a wide range of extensions, categorized and searchable to make finding what you're looking for easier. Once you find an extension you want to install, click on the "Get" button, and Edge will install it.

Leveraging extensions, you can tailor Microsoft Edge to your liking and make it a tool that works seamlessly with your workflow. One of my favorite extensions is the "Dark Reader," which turns websites into dark mode, reducing eye strain and providing a sleek appearance. Whether you're a designer, writer, or spend a lot of time on the web, there's an extension out there that will make your browsing experience more enjoyable and efficient.

Privacy Settings

Now, let's turn our attention to privacy settings in Microsoft Edge. Privacy has become a paramount concern in today's digital landscape, and Edge provides several features to help you protect your data and safeguard your online activities.

One of the most important features in Edge's privacy settings is the ability to control cookies. Cookies are small pieces of data stored on your device by websites you visit. While they can enhance your browsing experience by remembering preferences and login information, they can also be used to track your online behavior and gather personal information without your consent.

Microsoft Edge allows you to choose how cookies are handled. In the privacy settings, you can select from three options: "Block all cookies," "Don't block cookies," and "Block only third-party cookies." Choosing the right level of cookie control is crucial to balancing personalized browsing experiences and protecting your privacy. By default, Edge recommends blocking only third-party cookies, which helps prevent cross-site tracking without hindering your regular web interactions.

Tracking Prevention

Additionally, Edge offers a feature called Tracking Prevention, which is designed to block third-party trackers that could compromise your privacy by collecting data about your online activities. Tracking Prevention operates on three levels: Basic, Balanced, and Strict. Basic is the default setting and strikes a balance between privacy and compatibility, while Strict aims to provide maximum privacy protection by blocking most trackers. You can adjust the level of Tracking Prevention that best suits your needs by going to "Settings," then "Privacy, search, and services," and finally "Tracking Prevention."

For an extra layer of security, Microsoft Edge also offers the option to browse in InPrivate mode. When you open an InPrivate window, Edge will not save your browsing history, cookies, or site data. It's like browsing incognito, giving you peace of mind when you don't want your online activities to be visible to others who may use the same device.

As I reach the end of this subchapter on mastering the Microsoft Edge web browser, I am filled with a sense of accomplishment. My detailed exploration of tab management, extensions, and privacy settings has shed light on the powerful capabilities of Edge and inspired you to take full advantage of this robust browsing tool.

UNLEASHING CREATIVITY WITH PAINT 3D

As I delve deeper into the fascinating world of Windows 11, I am constantly amazed by the array of tools and applications it offers. In this chapter, we will explore the limitless possibilities of the Paint 3D app, a powerful tool that allows users to unleash their creativity through 3D modeling and editing.

1. Getting Started with Paint 3D

Before we embark on this creative journey, let's familiarize ourselves with the Paint 3D app. To open the app, click the

Start button and search for "Paint 3D." Once you open it, you will be greeted with a clean and user-friendly interface that invites you to explore your artistic genius.

2. Exploring the 3D Tools

One of the most exciting features of Paint 3D is its 3D modeling tools. With these tools, you can bring your imagination to life by creating three-dimensional objects. To begin, click the "3D shapes" button on the top menu. From here, you can choose from a wide range of pre-designed 3D shapes, such as cubes, spheres, cylinders, and more.

But why limit yourself to pre-designed shapes when you can create something truly unique? Paint 3D offers the option to start with a blank canvas and use the various 2D shapes to construct your masterpiece. You can even import existing 2D images and convert them into 3D objects, giving your creations a whole new dimension.

3. Using the Magic Select Tool

To further enhance your creativity, Paint 3D provides a magical tool called the "Magic Select." This tool isolates objects from images and manipulates them in a three-dimensional space. Imagine removing a person from a photograph and placing them in a different setting. With the Magic Select tool, the possibilities are endless.

To use the Magic Select tool, click the "Magic Select" button in the top menu and draw a rough outline around the object you wish to extract. Paint 3D's advanced algorithms will then detect the object and create a selection. You can refine this selection by using the "Add" or "Remove" buttons, ensuring that only the desired object is isolated.

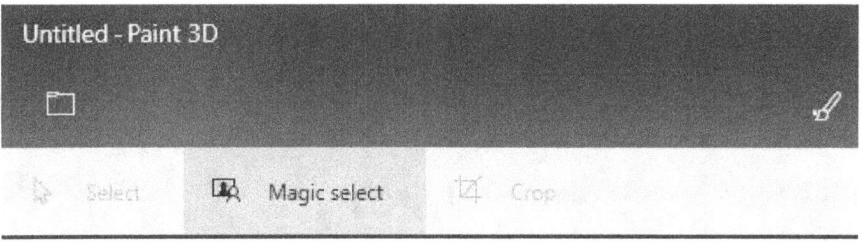

4. Texturing and Coloring Your Creations

Now that you have created your 3D objects, it's time to add some life. Paint 3D allows you to apply textures and colors to your creations, making them visually compelling and realistic. To access the texturing options, click the "3D objects" button in the top menu and select the object you wish to texture.

Once you have chosen your desired object, a new " Textures " tab will appear in the right sidebar. Here, you can choose from various pre-designed textures or even import your own. From woodgrains to metals, the possibilities are vast. Furthermore, you can adjust the scale and rotation of the textures to achieve the desired effect.

To add colors to your objects, navigate to the "Brushes" tab in the sidebar. Here, you will find an assortment of brushes, colors, and gradients to choose from. Select the desired color and start painting your masterpiece. With each stroke of your virtual brush, your creation will come to life in vibrant hues.

5. Adding Depth with Layers

To add depth and complexity to your creations, Paint 3D offers a layering system. Think of layers as transparent sheets stacked on top of each other. Each layer can be edited individually, allowing you to make changes without affecting the rest of your composition.

To add a new layer, click on the "Layers" button in the top menu and select "New." You can then experiment with different brushes, colors, and textures without worrying about permanently changing your original work. Layers provide the flexibility and freedom to explore your artistic vision without limitations.

6. Combining Paint 3D with Other Windows 11 Apps

While Paint 3D is a powerful tool, it becomes even more transformative when combined with other Windows 11 apps. You can seamlessly integrate your 3D creations into other apps such as PowerPoint, Word, or 3D Builder. This allows you to incorporate your unique designs into presentations, documents, or even 3D prints.

Let your imagination run wild as you explore the endless possibilities of Windows 11's creative ecosystem. Paint 3D serves as a gateway to a world where innovation and artistic expression merge, unleashing a new level of creativity.

7. Sharing Your Masterpieces

Art is meant to be shared, and Paint 3D makes it effortless to showcase your creations with the world. You can save your masterpiece as an image or 3D model with just a few clicks. Paint 3D supports various file formats, allowing you to share your work on social media, websites, or even collaborate with others.

Additionally, Paint 3D offers a built-in community where you can explore and be inspired by the work of other talented artists. You can upload your creations to the community, receive feedback, and interact with fellow artists. The possibilities for collaboration and growth are boundless.

In conclusion, Paint 3D is a remarkable tool that empowers beginners and experienced artists alike to unleash their creativity in the world of three-dimensional design. Its intuitive interface, versatile tools, and integration with other Windows 11 apps offer a platform for endless exploration and artistic expression. So, dive into the world of Paint 3D and let your imagination soar. Your next masterpiece awaits.

STAYING CONNECTED WITH THE MAIL AND CALENDAR APPS

Introduction to the Mail and Calendar Apps:

We live in a fast-paced, interconnected world, where keeping track of emails and appointments can often feel overwhelming. Windows 11 aims to simplify this process with its Mail and Calendar apps. Whether you're a student managing multiple assignments and deadlines or professional juggling meetings and tasks, these apps provide a centralized hub for all your communication and scheduling needs.

Setting Up Your Email Accounts:

Setting up your email accounts before diving into the Mail and Calendar apps' functionalities is essential. Windows 11 supports various email providers such as Outlook, Gmail, Yahoo, and more. By inputting your email credentials, Windows 11 securely connects to your mailbox and brings all your messages and contacts together in one place.

Navigating the Mail App:

Once your accounts are set up, it's time to explore the Mail app's interface. The Mail app offers a clean and user-friendly design, making it easy to navigate through your emails effortlessly. The interface displays your inbox on the left, allowing you to access folders, contacts, and filters quickly. On the right, you have a preview pane that displays the content of an email.

Composing and Sending Emails:

Now that you can access your emails, it's crucial to understand how to compose and send messages effectively. The Mail app provides a straightforward interface for composing emails. You have various formatting options to make your email visually appealing, such as font selection, text alignment, and bullet points.

Additionally, you can attach files or images directly from your computer, making it convenient to share documents or pictures with your contacts.

Organizing and Managing Your Inbox:

With the volume of emails we receive daily, it's essential to have a systematic approach to organizing and managing our inboxes. The Mail app offers features like flagging, categorizing, and sorting, allowing you to prioritize and stay on top of your emails. Flags can be reminders for important messages, while categories help you group similar emails together. You can also sort your inbox by date, sender, or subject to quickly locate specific emails.

Utilizing Filters and Folders:

Filters and folders are powerful tools within the Mail app to streamline your email management. Filters allow you to automatically sort incoming emails based on specific criteria, such as sender or subject. This way, you can set up filters to direct newsletters to a designated folder or mark emails from certain contacts as important. Folders, however, enable you to create a personalized structure within your inbox to categorize and store emails.

Creating and Managing Calendar Events:

Beyond managing emails, the Calendar app in Windows 11 enables you to create and track appointments and events seamlessly. You can schedule meetings, set reminders, and even invite attendees with just a few clicks. The Calendar app offers various views, including day, week, month, and year, allowing you to visualize your schedule in a way that suits your needs best.

Syncing Your Calendar with Other Devices:

In today's interconnected world, relying on multiple devices to stay organized is common. Windows 11 offers synchronization capabilities, ensuring your calendar events are accessible across all your devices. By linking your Microsoft account, you can effortlessly view and edit your calendar from your computer, tablet, or smartphone, providing a consistent and up-to-date view of your schedule.

Collaborating and Sharing Calendars:

Whether coordinating team meetings or organizing family events, the Calendar app simplifies collaboration by allowing you to share your calendar with others. You can grant specific individuals or groups access to view or edit your events, making coordinating schedules easier and avoiding miscommunications.

Additional Tips and Tricks:

As you become more comfortable with the Mail and Calendar apps in Windows 11, several additional tips and tricks can help you further streamline your experience. For instance, you can customize the app's settings to personalize your email signature, set up automatic replies, or establish rules to manage incoming emails more efficiently. Additionally, you can explore the integration of other productivity tools, such as Microsoft To Do or OneNote, to enhance your workflow.

Conclusion:

In this subchapter, we have explored the Mail and Calendar apps in Windows 11 and how they can effectively help you manage your emails and schedule. From setting up email accounts to composing messages, organizing your inbox, and creating calendar events, we have covered the essential aspects of these apps. Utilizing the features and functionalities offered lets you stay connected, organized, and efficient in your daily communication and scheduling tasks.

CHAPTER 4: SECURING AND MAINTAINING YOUR WINDOWS 11 SYSTEM

PROTECTING YOUR SYSTEM WITH WINDOWS DEFENDER

Windows Defender is an antivirus and antispyware program that works silently in the background, constantly monitoring your system for malicious activities and attempting to remove them. It provides real-time protection against viruses, malware, ransomware, and other malicious software that can harm your system.

To access Windows Defender, click the Start button and type "Windows Defender" in the search bar. Click on the Windows Defender Security Center to open the security dashboard.

Once you open Windows Defender, you'll be greeted with an overview of your system's security status. It will display information about the latest scan, virus and threat protection, firewall and network protection, app and browser control, device performance and health, and family options. It's important to regularly check this dashboard to ensure everything is up to date and there are no potential threats to your system.

The first aspect of protection that Windows Defender offers is virus and threat protection. By default, it automatically scans your system regularly to check for potential threats. However, you can manually initiate a scan by clicking the "Quick Scan" or "Full Scan" options.

A quick scan focuses on the most vulnerable areas of your system, such as the system files and running processes, giving you a quick overview of any potential threats. On the other hand, a full scan thoroughly examines every file and folder on your system, leaving no stone unturned. It is recommended to perform a full scan periodically to ensure comprehensive security.

Windows Defender also provides an option called "Windows Defender Offline Scan," which allows you to scan your system for malicious software before it boots up. This is particularly useful in case your system has been infected and your regular scans aren't able to remove the threat. To perform an offline scan, go to the "Virus and threat protection" tab in the Windows Defender Security Center and click "Advanced Scan." Select "Windows Defender Offline Scan" from there and follow the onscreen instructions.

Firewall and network protection are another key aspects of Windows Defender. A firewall acts as a barrier between your system and the internet, monitoring incoming and outgoing network traffic to detect and block any unauthorized connections or suspicious activities. Windows Defender's built-in firewall automatically protects your system, blocking potentially harmful connections and preventing unauthorized access to your computer.

App and browser control is an essential feature of Windows Defender, as it helps protect you from malicious apps and unsafe websites. Windows Defender analyzes the behaviour of apps and files as they execute on your system, looking for any signs of suspicious activity. It also provides real-time protection while browsing the internet, blocking known malicious websites and warning you about potentially unsafe ones.

Device performance and health is another important aspect that Windows Defender focuses on. It monitors the overall health of your system, keeping an eye on factors like battery life, storage capacity, and device drivers. It also alerts you if any of these aspects need attention or if there are any issues with system updates or Windows security settings.

Finally, Windows Defender offers family options that enable you to manage the security settings for your family members' accounts. You can set up parental controls, limit screen time, and monitor your child's online activities to ensure they are safe and secure while using their Windows 11 devices. This feature provides peace of mind for parents, knowing they have control over their child's digital experiences.

In conclusion, Windows Defender is indispensable for protecting your Windows 11 system from potential threats. Its comprehensive set of security features, including virus and threat protection, firewall and network protection, app and browser control, device performance and health monitoring, and family options, ensure that your system and your personal data are safe from the ever-looming cyber threats. By regularly utilizing and updating Windows Defender, you can make sure that your Windows 11 experience remains secure and worry-free. Remember, it's better to be safe than sorry in this digital age.

OPTIMIZING PERFORMANCE WITH SYSTEM MAINTENANCE

Disk Cleanup

To begin, let's talk about disk cleanup. Over time, our systems tend to accumulate unnecessary files, temporary data, and other clutter. This takes up valuable space on your hard drive and slows down your system. The good news is that Windows 11 comes with a built-in Disk Cleanup tool that makes the process of removing this digital debris a breeze.

Launching the Disk Cleanup tool is as simple as opening the Start menu, typing "Disk Cleanup," and selecting the appropriate result. Once inside the tool, you'll be presented with a list of file categories to choose from. These categories represent different files that can be safely removed to free up space.

For instance, the "Temporary files" category should be checked by default, as it contains all the temporary files generated by various applications and can quickly accumulate over time. The "System files" category also allows you to remove unnecessary system files such as Windows Update leftovers, error reports, and Windows upgrade log files.

After selecting the desired categories, click on "OK" to begin the cleanup process. This can take several minutes, depending on how much data is removed. Once complete, you'll be amazed at how much space you've freed up and how much smoother your system will run.

Defragmentation

Moving on to defragmentation, this process aims to optimize the placement of files on your hard drive, ensuring quicker access times for your frequently used applications and files. In Windows 11, the defragmentation tool is aptly called "Optimize Drives" and is just a few clicks away.

To start the optimization process, open the Start menu, type "Optimize Drives," and select the corresponding result. This will bring up a window displaying your system's available drives. Select the drive you wish to optimize (typically the C: drive) and click the "Optimize" button.

Windows 11 will then analyze the drive's status and determine whether or not an optimization is required. If optimization is needed, the tool will rearrange the files on your drive, minimizing fragmentation and improving performance. Like disk cleanup, the optimization process may take some time to complete, so it's best to schedule it when you won't need to use your system intensively.

The Troubleshoot Feature

In addition to disk cleanup and defragmentation, Windows 11 offers a range of other maintenance tools that can help troubleshoot common issues and keep your system in peak condition. For example, the "Troubleshoot" feature can automatically scan and fix problems related to your network connection, audio devices, and Windows Update.

To access the Troubleshoot feature, open the Start menu, type "Troubleshoot," and select the relevant result. This will bring up a list of troubleshooting options you can explore based on the specific issues you may be facing. From there, follow the onscreen instructions and let

Windows 11 guide you through the troubleshooting process.

Task Manager

Additionally, Windows 11 includes a powerful tool called "Task Manager" that allows you to monitor and manage the applications and processes running on your system. By opening the Task Manager (pressing Ctrl + Shift + Esc or right-clicking on the taskbar and selecting "Task Manager"), you can identify resource-hungry applications causing performance issues and close them if necessary.

Furthermore, the Task Manager provides detailed information about various system performance metrics such as CPU usage, memory usage, and disk activity. This information can be invaluable when troubleshooting performance issues or identifying processes slowing down your system.

By utilizing the system maintenance tools that Windows 11 offers, you can easily optimise your system's performance and troubleshoot common issues. Whether performing regular disk cleanups, defragmenting your hard drive, or using the troubleshooting features, investing a little time in system maintenance can go a long way in ensuring a smooth and efficient Windows 11 experience. So go ahead, embark on this journey of optimization, and unlock the full potential of your Windows 11 system. Happy computing!

BACKING UP AND RESTORING YOUR FILES IN WINDOWS 11

Before we dive into the nitty-gritty of creating backups, let's take a moment to understand the importance of backing up your files. Imagine you have spent countless hours meticulously organizing your photo collection or meticulously crafting a novel. A sudden hardware failure or a malicious malware attack can instantly wipe out everything, leaving you devastated and powerless. By creating regular backups, you can safeguard your data and ensure an extra layer of protection against such unexpected calamities.

Windows 11 introduces a seamless backup and restore experience, offering users an intuitive interface and robust functionality. To start the process, navigate to the Settings app by clicking the Start menu and selecting the gear icon. Within the Settings app, locate the System category and click on it. Here, you will find a tab named 'Backup' with all the necessary tools to safeguard your files.

Once you've clicked on the 'Backup' tab, you will be presented with various options related to file backup, including 'Backup devices,' 'Backup settings,' and 'Backup options.' Let's explore each option to ensure you understand how to utilize the Windows 11 backup and restore features effectively.

The first step towards protecting your files is connecting an external storage device, such as a USB or an external hard drive, to your computer. This device will serve as the destination where your files will be backed up. Windows 11 allows you to use either a traditional HDD or a modern SSD, both of which offer ample storage capacity and reliable performance.

To add a backup device, click the 'Add a drive' option under the 'Backup devices' section. Windows 11 will detect any external drives connected to your computer and display them as available options. Select the desired device, and Windows 11 will automatically configure it for backup purposes. You can add multiple backup devices if needed.

Now that you have successfully added a backup device, let's configure the backup settings. Under the 'Backup settings' section, you will find an option called 'Automatically back up my files.' By enabling this feature, Windows 11 will automatically back up your files regularly, ensuring you have the most up-to-date copy of your data. This real-time backup eliminates losing any recently created or modified files.

Click the 'More options' button to customise your backup settings further. Here, you can specify how often you want Windows 11 to perform backups, choose specific folders or libraries to include or exclude from the backup, or specify a network location as your backup destination. Windows

11 offers flexibility, allowing you to tailor the backup process to your unique needs.

Once you have configured the backup settings to your liking, it's time to initiate the backup process. By clicking the 'Back up now' button, Windows 11 will start creating a backup of your files. The duration of this process depends on the size of your data and the speed of your storage device. You can monitor the progress through the backup status indicator, ensuring everything runs smoothly.

Windows 11 also provides a comprehensive view of your backup history. You can access this information by clicking the 'More options' button under the 'Backup options' section and selecting 'Backup history.' Here, you will find a list of all the previous backups, their creation dates, and the size of the backup sets. This detailed overview allows you to keep track of your backup activities and evaluate the effectiveness of your backup strategy.

Now that we have thoroughly explored creating backups in Windows 11, let's discuss how to restore your files when needed. Whether you accidentally delete an important document or find some files corrupted, Windows 11 provides a straightforward method to recover your data and bring it back to its original state.

To initiate the file restoration process, return to the 'Backup' tab within the Settings app and click the 'More options' button under the 'Backup options' section. You will find the 'Restore files from a current backup' option here. Clicking on this will open the File History app, which serves as the control center for all your restoration needs.

Within the File History app, you will be presented with a timeline view of your backups. You can navigate this timeline to identify the specific backup from which you want to restore your files. Once you have selected the desired timestamp, you can browse through the backup set, explore individual folders, and locate the files you wish to restore.

To restore a file, select it and click the 'Restore' button. Windows 11 will retrieve the selected file from the backup and place it in its original location on your computer's hard drive. If you want to restore multiple files simultaneously, you can hold the Ctrl key while selecting each file. This convenient feature saves you precious time and effort when dealing with many files.

In addition to restoring individual files, Windows 11 offers the option to restore an entire folder or drive. By clicking on the 'Restore all files' option within the File History app, you can restore an entire folder hierarchy, ensuring that no single file is left behind. Similarly, if you want to restore an entire drive, such as your C: drive, you can navigate to the drive in the File History app and click the 'Restore' button.

It is worth mentioning that Windows 11 retains multiple versions of your files within the backup set, allowing you to restore older versions if needed. This can be particularly useful if you want to revert to a previous document iteration or recover a file that has been unintentionally modified or deleted. The File History app provides an easy-to-use interface for accessing and restoring these earlier versions.

In conclusion, creating backups and restoring files is essential to maintaining data integrity and safeguarding your valuable files. Windows 11 simplifies this process by providing a comprehensive backup and restore feature set within its user-friendly interface. Utilizing the step-by-step guide outlined in this subchapter, you can create regular backups of your files, configure custom backup settings, and effortlessly restore your data whenever needed. Remember, by practicing proactive data management, you can minimize the impact of potential data loss and ensure that your files are always protected.

CHAPTER 5: ADVANCED TIPS AND TRICKS FOR WINDOWS 11

MASTERING KEYBOARD SHORTCUTS AND GESTURES

As I begin my journey into the world of keyboard shortcuts, I am met with a sense of excitement and curiosity. Windows 11 offers many shortcuts that can be customized to suit individual preferences. One of the most basic shortcuts is the iconic "Ctrl +C" and "Ctrl + V" combination for copying and pasting. Since their inception, these shortcuts have been a cornerstone of computer usage, allowing users to duplicate and move text or files effortlessly. However, Windows 11 takes it a step further by introducing more advanced shortcuts that can expedite various tasks.

For instance, pressing the "Windows key + D" brings me to the desktop, instantly minimizing all open windows. This simple shortcut is invaluable when I need to quickly access a file or application without the clutter of multiple open windows. Alternatively, I can press "Windows key + L" to lock my computer, providing quick security when I step away momentarily.

Another set of shortcuts that Windows 11 introduces revolves around multitasking and window management.

As I become familiar with these gestures, my productivity soars. For example, pressing "Windows key + Left Arrow" or "Windows key + Right Arrow" snaps the active window to the left or right side of the screen, allowing me to work with two windows side by side. A simple "Windows key + Up Arrow" maximizes the active window to fill the entire screen, while "Windows key + Down Arrow" minimizes or restores the window. These shortcuts enable me to arrange and manage windows, making multitasking a breeze effortlessly.

Amidst my exploration, I discovered the power of touch gestures in Windows 11. With the advent of touchscreen devices, performing tasks with the flick of a finger has become a preferred method for many users. Windows 11 capitalizes on this trend by introducing a range of intuitive and efficient touch gestures.

The first gesture that catches my attention is the swipe from the left edge of the screen towards the center, which reveals the Task View. This feature displays all open windows, making switching between applications or documents easy. Similarly, swiping in from the right edge of the screen reveals the Action Center, where I have quick access to various system settings and notifications. These gestures mimic the functionality of traditional buttons but provide a more seamless and visually appealing experience.

Navigating through open applications is made even simpler with the ability to swipe up from the taskbar. This action reveals the "Taskbar preview," displaying all active applications. I can easily switch between windows from here, ensuring a smoother workflow.

In addition to these touch gestures, Windows 11 also introduces a number of new gestures specifically designed for touchscreen devices. For instance, a three-finger swipe-up reveals the new Desktop Overview, presenting a bird's eye view of all open windows, allowing for effortless navigation and organization. Furthermore, a three-finger swipe down minimizes all open windows, providing a clear workspace to focus on the task at hand.

Windows Subsystem for Linux, or WSL, is another area where keyboard shortcuts can significantly enhance the user experience. WSL allows users to run various Linux distributions on Windows, bridging the gap between different operating systems. With the integration of WSL in Windows 11, mastering the keyboard shortcuts associated with this feature proves to be invaluable for those who frequently work in a Linux environment. For instance, pressing "Ctrl + ` " (the backtick key) opens a terminal window, allowing for seamless access to the Linux shell. This shortcut eliminates the need to navigate through menus or search for the correct application to launch a terminal, saving valuable time and effort.

As I continue exploring the realm of keyboard shortcuts and touch gestures in Windows 11, I am astounded by their myriad possibilities. From enhancing productivity to simplifying navigation, mastering these shortcuts and gestures truly transforms how I interact with my computer. I find myself effortlessly gliding through tasks, accomplishing more in less time. Windows 11 has revolutionized the user interface concept, bringing efficiency and elegance to the forefront.

In conclusion, this subchapter has introduced readers to the world of keyboard shortcuts and touch gestures in Windows 11. We have explored a range of shortcuts, from the basic to the advanced, that can expedite various tasks and enhance productivity. Additionally, we have delved into the world of touch gestures, discovering how they provide a seamless and visually appealing way to navigate through the operating system. Whether it's the swipe of a finger or the press of a key, mastering these shortcuts and gestures empowers users to unlock the full potential of Windows 11 and embark on a journey of efficiency and productivity. So dive in and explore the vast landscape of shortcuts and gestures available in Windows 11. Your computer experience will never be the same again.

EXPLORING HIDDEN FEATURES AND SETTINGS

When it comes to exploring hidden features and settings, the first thing that comes to mind is the Action Center. Previously known as the Notification Center, the Action Center in Windows 11 has been redesigned to offer a more comprehensive view of all your notifications and quick-access settings. To access the Action Center, click on the icon in the bottom right corner of the taskbar, or use the keyboard shortcut Win + A. Once opened, you will be greeted with many options, from brightness controls to network settings. However, most users might need to be made aware of the ability to customize the Action Center to their liking. By clicking on the three dots at the top of the Action Center, you can access the settings and personalize what notifications are shown, the layout of the Quick Actions section, and even choose whether or not to display the brightness slider.

Moving on, another hidden gem in Windows 11 is the revamped Microsoft Store. This new version of the Microsoft Store brings a fresh look and introduces the ability to install Android apps, giving you access to a wider range of software. To do this, open the Microsoft Store and click on the Android Apps section at the top. From there, you can search for your favorite Android apps and install them on your Windows 11 device. This integration of Android apps within Windows 11 opens up a world of possibilities and allows you to extend the functionality of your device.

One of my favorite hidden features in Windows 11 is the new Snap Layouts and Snap Groups feature. Snap Layouts allows you to easily organize and work with multiple windows on your desktop. To use this feature, drag a window to any edge of your screen, and it will automatically snap into place, taking up a portion of the screen. You can then select another window and snap it into a different position, allowing you to create a multitasking environment tailored to your needs. What's even more impressive is the ability to create Snap Groups. By clicking on the maximize button of a window, you can create a group consisting of multiple windows that you frequently use together. This allows you to quickly switch between different sets of windows without the hassle of manually rearranging them every time.

Next on our exploration journey is the hidden world of virtual desktops. Virtual desktops have been a part of Windows for quite some time now, but Windows 11 takes it to a new level. To access virtual desktops, click the Task View button on the taskbar or use the keyboard shortcut Win + Tab. This will open up the Task View interface, where you can see all your virtual desktops and the open windows within them. What sets Windows 11 apart is the ability to personalize each virtual desktop by giving it a custom name and background. This allows you to create separate workspaces for different tasks or projects, keeping your workflow organized and efficient. To add a new virtual desktop, click on the New Desktop option at the top of the Task View interface.

As we delve deeper into the hidden features and settings of Windows 11, let's not forget about the power of personalization. Windows 11 offers a plethora of options to customize your desktop, from changing the wallpaper to modifying the appearance of the taskbar. To access the personalization settings, right-click on your desktop and select Personalize from the context menu. From there, you can choose from various pre-installed wallpapers or set your image as the background. Moreover, Windows 11 introduces the concept of "themes, " a collection of wallpapers, accent colors, and sounds that can be easily applied to give your desktop a fresh look. To create your theme, navigate to the Themes section of the personalization settings and click the Create new theme button. From there, you can mix and match different wallpapers, colors, and sounds to create your personalized theme.

Another hidden feature in Windows 11 that can significantly enhance your user experience is the Power & Sleep settings. These settings allow you to specify how long your computer remains active before going to sleep or turning off the display. To access the Power & Sleep settings, click the Start button and select Settings. From there, navigate to the System section and click Power & Sleep. Here, you can customize the sleep and display timeout settings according to your preferences. If you want to conserve battery life, you can set a shorter timeout duration, while if you prefer your computer to stay active for extended periods, you can opt for a longer duration. Windows 11 also introduces the ability to customize the behavior when you close the laptop lid, allowing you to define whether your computer should sleep, shut down, or do nothing.

One feature that often goes unnoticed by Windows users is the Clipboard History feature. Traditionally, the clipboard was limited to storing only the most recent item copied or cut. However, with the Clipboard History feature in Windows 11, you can now access a history of your copied items and even pin frequently used items for quick access. To access the Clipboard History, press the Win + V keyboard shortcut. This will open a floating window that displays all your copied items. You can scroll through the list to find the item you want to paste or use the search bar to locate a specific item quickly. Additionally, if you come across an item you frequently use, you can pin it to the clipboard history for easy access.

In conclusion, Windows 11 is not just a visually stunning operating system; it is also packed with hidden features and settings that can greatly enhance your user experience and provide additional customization options. From the revamped Action Center to integrating Android apps in the Microsoft Store, Windows 11 opens up a world of possibilities for users. Whether organizing windows with Snap Layouts and Snap Groups, creating personalized virtual desktops, or customizing your desktop with themes, Windows 11 empowers you to tailor your computing experience to your liking. So take the time to explore the hidden features and settings of Windows 11, and unlock the full potential of this remarkable operating system.

TROUBLESHOOTING COMMON WINDOWS 11 ISSUES

1. Slow Performance:

One common issue that many Windows 11 users face is slow performance. This can be frustrating, significantly impacting your productivity and overall experience. Thankfully, there are several steps you can take to address this problem.

Firstly, check if any unnecessary background processes are running on your system. These processes consume system resources and can degrade performance. By accessing the Task Manager, you can identify the resource-intensive processes and close or adjust their settings to minimize their impact.

Another potential cause of slow performance is insufficient storage space on your hard drive. Windows 11 requires a certain amount of free space to function optimally. Remove unnecessary files or programs to free up space if your drive is near capacity.

Additionally, performing regular disk cleanup and defragmentation can help maintain system performance. Both tools can be accessed by typing "Disk Cleanup" and "Defragment and Optimize Drives" in the search bar. By running these tools, you can remove temporary files and optimize the data placement on your hard drive.

2. Blue Screen of Death (BSOD):

The notorious Blue Screen of Death, or BSOD, can be terrifying for any Windows 11 user. This screen typically appears when your system encounters a critical error, forcing your computer to restart to prevent further damage. Resolving this issue requires some troubleshooting skills.

One potential cause of the BSOD is outdated or incompatible drivers. Device drivers are essential software components that allow hardware devices to communicate with your operating system. If a driver is outdated or incompatible, it can lead to system instability and crashes.

To address this issue, you should ensure that all your drivers are up to date. Visit the manufacturer's website or use a driver update utility to download and install the latest drivers for your hardware devices. Additionally, consider disabling any recently installed drivers or rolling back to a previous version to identify the specific driver causing the problem.

Another potential cause of the BSOD is faulty hardware. If you have recently installed new hardware or made changes to your system, it's worth checking if these components function correctly. You can do this by removing or disabling the hardware and observing if the BSOD persists. If the problem disappears after removing a particular component, you may need to replace or repair it.

3. Connectivity Issues:

Issues with internet connectivity or connecting to other devices are also common in Windows 11. These problems can stem from various sources, but there are a few troubleshooting steps you can take to address them.

Firstly, check if your Wi-Fi or Ethernet adapter is functioning correctly. You can do this by accessing the Device Manager and ensuring no warning signs or exclamation marks are next to your network adapters. If there is an issue with the adapter, you can try reinstalling the driver or using the device's troubleshooting feature to resolve it.

If you are experiencing Wi-Fi connectivity issues, try restarting your router and modem. This simple step often resolves temporary connectivity problems caused by network congestion or device conflicts. Additionally, if you frequently connect to public Wi-Fi networks, consider using a virtual private network (VPN) to ensure a secure and stable connection.

For issues related to connecting to other devices, such as printers or external monitors, ensure that the necessary drivers are installed correctly. If the device is not recognized or functioning as expected, try reinstalling or updating the drivers to the latest version.

4. Application Compatibility:

Windows 11 introduces various new features and improvements but may also create compatibility issues with older applications. If you encounter errors or crashes when running certain programs, here are some steps you can take to address the problem.

Firstly, try running the application in compatibility mode. Right-click on the program's icon or executable file, select "Properties," and navigate to the "Compatibility" tab. From there, you can choose to run the program in compatibility mode for a previous version of Windows. This can often resolve compatibility issues by emulating the environment in which the application was initially designed to run.

If running the program in compatibility mode does not resolve the issue, you can try running it as an administrator. Right-click the program's icon or executable file, select "Run as administrator," and check if the problem persists. Running the application with elevated privileges can sometimes bypass compatibility issues.

In some cases, you may need to seek alternative solutions. If a program is incompatible with Windows 11, consider searching for a similar program that meets your needs. Many developers release updated software versions to ensure compatibility with the latest operating systems.

By following these troubleshooting steps, you can address common issues that may arise while using Windows 11. Remember to remain patient and diligent throughout the process, as troubleshooting often requires trial and error. You can ensure a smooth and uninterrupted computing experience with these skills and knowledge.

CONCLUSION

"In conclusion, 'Windows 11 for Beginners 2024' was designed with the novice computer user in mind, aiming to provide a solid foundation for understanding and navigating the Windows 11 operating system. Throughout this book, we've covered essential topics such as the Start Menu, file management, web browsing, and personalization. We hope this guide has demystified Windows 11 for you and helped you gain confidence in using your computer effectively.

As you wrap up your journey through this book, remember that learning is an ongoing process. Windows 11 is a dynamic operating system, and there will always be new features and updates to explore. We encourage you to continue practicing what you've learned and to stay curious about the possibilities that Windows 11 offers.

Additionally, don't hesitate to seek additional resources, online communities, and support if you have questions or encounter challenges in your Windows 11 journey. Technology is a tool that can enhance our lives in countless ways, and Windows 11 is a versatile platform that can be customized to suit your needs and preferences.

Thank you for choosing 'Windows 11 for Beginners 2024' as your starting point in Windows computing. We hope you feel more comfortable and capable when using your computer, and we wish you success in all your digital endeavors. Remember, with Windows 11, the possibilities are endless, and you are in control of your computing experience."

If you enjoyed this book, check out these other titles. Happy reading!

www.ingramcontent.com/pod-product-compliance
Lightning Source LLC
Chambersburg PA
CBHW062238290526
45794CB00006B/2329